From a Father's Heart

Guidance for the Journey of Life

Stan E. DeKoven, Ph.D.

From a Father's Heart:
Guidance for the Journey of Life

From a Father's Heart

*Guidance for the
Journey of Life*

Copyright © 1996

By Dr. Stan E. DeKoven

Second Edition 2005

ISBN: 978-1-61529-073-4

Third Edition 2013

All rights in this book are reserved world-wide.

No part of this book may be reproduced in any manner without the written permission of the author, except in brief quotations embodied in critical articles or reviews.

For information on reordering please contact:

Vision Publishing
1672 Main St., E109
Ramona, CA 92065
(760) 789-4700
www.booksbyvision.com

Dedication

For

Rebecca Ann

And

Rachel Elizabeth

My Precious Beautiful Daughters

*From a Father's Heart:
Guidance for the Journey of Life*

From a Father's Heart

A PERSONAL NOTE
From a Father's or Mother's Heart
(Space for personal dedication)

From a Father's Heart:
Guidance for the Journey of Life

Table of Contents

Chapter One 9

Chapter Two 23

Chapter Three 29

Chapter Four 35

Chapter Five 41

Chapter Six 55

Chapter Seven 71

Conclusion 75

Introduction

Chapter One

Introduction

To say I have looked forward to writing this work is mostly true, though partially not. To write this means that my children are grown, my wife[1] and I are facing our transition towards mid-life and my role as dad is no longer what it was. I am excited about the future, with apprehension of the unsure. For my children have only begun to traverse adulthood; it was only yesterday that they were a bundle of potential in mom's and dad's loving arms. Such are the seasons of life, ever marching, always the same and ever changing.

As I said, I have looked forward to writing down my reflections, not on the past, but on the future. My purpose is to provide (howbeit, at times with immense protectiveness, sentimentality and one man's opinion) what is essential for the remainder of a child's journey to maturity. Every thing learned, all experience both good and bad, every positive and negative example from significant people are primary preparation for the fulfillment of a God given plan. Though God's plan for man is unique and individual, it is not

---

[1] Sadly, my wife of 26 years, Karen went home to be with the Lord on January 24, 2000. She is sorely missed by all who knew and loved her.

Introduction

individualistic or independent from others. Patterns and examples from God's Word, advice from Biblical sages, mixed with practical application, if accepted and acted upon, leads to wisdom.

The why of my writing is quite simple. I desperately care for my children and have always desired to lay a foundation for successful living. This desire carries far beyond my children…my hope is to positively impact many other children, on behalf of contentious parents everywhere. You see, I have often wondered what my life would have been like if I (at least) would have had clearer and more comprehensive information and guidance from God's Word to make my choices. Certainly, I had some, from parents who loved me, who provided all they could for our care, and my siblings. All good parents, and mine were good, do their best in their role. A primary role of a father is to transmit/transfer history, essential components of life, from generation to generation. Historically, this has been done orally through the story telling of family life.

Thus, as a scribe did in the Old Testament, I am compelled to write what the Lord has whispered in my ear, through his Word, kind friends and even enemies met along life's road. With this information, just perhaps, my life will have greater meaning, and provide a blessing for the next generation. Further, my progeny, both physically and spiritually, will have greater opportunity with lessened pitfalls. With these and many other thoughts in mind, the following essential concepts are offered to my daughters, now my granddaughters and grandson, and to sons and daughters everywhere, from a father's heart.

What is Essential?

Well, let's just dive into this...conception is essential. From a most significant, intimate, prayerfully planned and wonderful encounter, God brings forth life, the continuation of God's purpose for mankind. From such a small beginning, have all of us come.

It may seem as though chance plays a part in our existence. How often my children asked the question, "Why did God place us in the DeKoven family?" I'll never know. But, I'm certain they asked. At times the question seemed important, at times trite. All I know is, it was and is God's sovereign will for my children to have been born in our family, and others to theirs. No accident of evolution or mere act of passion, though the environment of sin and generational iniquities affect us all, caused my children, born in the image of God, to be in our family. They were born out of God's great design and foreknowledge, and have every potential for good or evil, hope or despair. What is essential? Conception, God, Fear of the Lord, family, love, faith, suffering (unfortunate but true). These essentials and many others will be presented over the next few pages.

> *"Come, you children, listen to me; I will teach you the fear of the LORD." (Psalms 34:11)*

There is no greater lesson to learn than a genuine awe and respect for God. In this past generation, God has become friend, supplier, even rescuer. He is and does these things, but He is so much more. If I could transmit anything to a young person starting their adult road, it would be to seek a full awareness of the awesomeness of God in his holiness, majesty and power. God's Word is full of descriptive pictures

Introduction

of God's greatness. The reason we as his people should always honor, revere and respect him is because of His marvelous grace and mercy towards us. Just a few examples might paint an adequate though woefully incomplete picture.

> *In the morning, O LORD, You will hear my voice; In the morning I will order my prayer to You and eagerly watch. (Psalm 5:3)*

How incredible to imagine that the God of the universe condescends to hear our voice in prayer and will answer us.

> *"All the ends of the earth will remember and turn to the LORD, and all the families of the nations will worship before You. For the kingdom is the LORD'S and He rules over the nations." (Psalm 22:27-28)*

> *"The earth is the LORD'S, and all it contains, the world, and those who dwell in it." (Psalm 24:1)*

> *Psalms 139:1 states, "O LORD, You have searched me and known me. You know when I sit down and when I rise up; you understand my thought from afar. You scrutinize my path and my lying down, and are intimately acquainted with all my ways. Even before there is*

a word on my tongue, Behold, O LORD, You know it all. You have enclosed me behind and before, and laid Your hand upon me. Such knowledge is too wonderful for me; it is too high, I cannot attain to it. Where can I go from Your Spirit? Or where can I flee from Your presence? If I ascend to heaven, You are there; If I make my bed in Sheol, behold, You are there. If I take the wings of the dawn, if I dwell in the remotest part of the sea, even there Your hand will lead me, and Your right hand will lay hold of me. If I say, "Surely the darkness will overwhelm me, and the light around me will be night." Even the darkness is not dark to You, and the night is as bright as the day. Darkness and light are alike to You. For You formed my inward parts; you wove me in my mother's womb. I will give thanks to You, for I am fearfully and wonderfully made; wonderful are Your works, and my soul knows it very well. My frame was not hidden from You, when I was made in secret, and skillfully wrought in the depths of the earth; Your eyes have seen my

Introduction

unformed substance; and in Your book were all written the days that were ordained for me, when as yet there was not one of them. How precious also are Your thoughts to me, O God! How vast is the sum of them! If I should count them, they would outnumber the sand. When I awake, I am still with You. O that You would slay the wicked, O God; Depart from me, therefore, men of bloodshed. For they speak against You wickedly, and Your enemies take Your name in vain. Do I not hate those who hate You, O LORD? And do I not loathe those who rise up against You? I hate them with the utmost hatred; they have become my enemies. Search me, O God, and know my heart; try me and know my anxious thoughts; and see if there be any hurtful way in me, and lead me in the everlasting way.

Job 38:1-13, Then the LORD answered Job out of the whirlwind and said, "Who is this that darkens counsel by words without knowledge? "Now gird up your loins like a man, and I will ask you, and you instruct Me! "Where were you when I laid the foundation of the earth? Tell Me, if you have understanding, who set its measurements? Since you know. Or who stretched the line on it? "On what were its bases sunk? Or who laid its cornerstone, when the morning stars sang together And all the sons of God shouted for joy? "Or who enclosed the sea with doors When, bursting forth, it went out from the womb; When I made a cloud its garment And thick darkness its swaddling band, And I placed boundaries on it And set a bolt and doors, and I said, 'Thus far you shall come, but no farther; And here shall your proud waves stop'? "Have you ever in your life commanded the morning, and caused the dawn to know its place, that it might take hold of the ends of the earth, and the wicked be shaken out of it?

How great is God? He is immeasurable, incomprehensible, yet knowable. God is love, full of grace and mercy, infinitely good. How great is man? Man is virtually nothing in comparison. Mankind is now and forever will be totally dependent upon God, the maker and sustainer of all life. To fear the Lord is the beginning of wisdom and knowledge. To obtain wisdom, which is essential for success in the future, is to respect God and his Word.

Another picture of God's greatness and our need for him is found in Proverbs 6:20-23.

Introduction

My son, observe the commandment of your father And do not forsake the teaching of your mother; Bind them continually on your heart; Tie them around your neck. When you walk about, they will guide you; When you sleep, they will watch over you; And when you awake, they will talk to you. For the commandment is a lamp and the teaching is light; And reproofs for discipline are the way of life."

The commandments and teachings are inclusive of the general words of truth from mom and dad, but most specifically from God's Word. Binding them to your heart comes through study, quiet reflection, meditation and prayer. As you allow God's Word to sink deeply into your heart, the Holy Spirit will guide, give protection, and sweetly speak to you from the Father's heart. Many times I have gone to sleep meditating on God and ruminating on a problem, only to awaken with a fresh answer and assurance of God's direction.

It takes discipline, often correction, to access the principles of God and his Word. Nevertheless, God really is as close as a whispered prayer.

It is important to remember that God does have a wonderful purpose for all of his children. The prophet Jeremiah echoes this truth in the 29th chapter of Jeremiah, verses 11-13:

"'For I know the plans that I have for you,' declares the LORD, 'plans for

> *welfare and not for calamity to give you a future and a hope. 'Then you will call upon Me and come and pray to Me, and I will listen to you. 'You will seek Me and find Me when you search for Me with all your heart.*

What a wonderful promise. Of course, God's plans for our daily existence do not always work out so smoothly. Each day is filled with challenges. But God has the blessed perspective of the beginning and end at a glance. He knows that ultimately all things do work together for good to them that love the Lord. (Romans 8:28)

In light of His plans for us, the way to accomplish His plan is out- lined in His instruction to Israel, in Deuteronomy 6:1-9:

> *"Now this is the commandment, the statutes and the judgments which the LORD your God has commanded me to teach you, that you might do them in the land where you are going over to possess it, so that you and your son and your grandson might fear the LORD your God, to keep all His statutes and His commandments which I command you, all the days of your life, and that your days may be prolonged. O Israel, you should listen and be careful to do it, that it may be well with you and that you may multiply greatly, just as the LORD, the God of your fathers, has*

promised you, in a land flowing with milk and honey. Hear, O Israel! The LORD is our God, the LORD is one! "You shall love the LORD your God with all your heart and with all your soul and with all your might. These words, which I am commanding you today, shall be on your heart. You shall teach them diligently to your sons and shall talk of them when you sit in your house and when you walk by the way and when you lie down and when you rise up. You shall bind them as a sign on your hand and they shall be as frontals on your forehead. You shall write them on the doorposts of your house and on your gates."

The results of following His patterns are seen in Deuteronomy 11:18-28:

"You shall therefore impress these words of mine on your heart and on your soul; and you shall bind them as a sign on your hand, and they shall be as frontals on your forehead. You shall teach them to your sons, talking of them when you sit in your house and when you walk along the road and when you lie down and when you rise

up. *You shall write them on the doorposts of your house and on your gates, so that your days and the days of your sons may be multiplied on the land which the LORD swore to your fathers to give them, as long as the heavens remain above the earth. For if you are careful to keep all this commandment which I am commanding you to do, to love the LORD your God, to walk in all His ways and hold fast to him, then the LORD will drive out all these nations from before you, and you will dispossess nations greater and mightier than you. Every place on which the sole of your foot treads shall be yours; your border will be from the wilderness to Lebanon, and from the river, the river Euphrates, as far as the western sea. No man will be able to stand before you; the LORD your God will lay the dread of you and the fear of you on all the land on which you set foot, as He has spoken to you. See, I am setting before you today a blessing and a curse: the blessing, if you listen to the commandments of the LORD your God, which I am commanding you today; and the curse, if you do not*

Introduction

listen to the commandments of the LORD your God, but turn aside from the way which I am commanding you today, by following other gods which you have not known.

The biblical mandate is for fathers especially (of course, mothers are included) to teach children about God, His ways and requirements, His blessings and warnings. The method of this teaching is a daily lifestyle more than classroom instruction.

One of my concerns is that my life has lacked a consistent witness of the grace and mercy of God and that the church (especially in America) has been so focused on form and materialism that this simple yet profound requirement has been neglected. I suppose what I am saying is that If I could start over I would spend much more time taking walks, going to parks, enjoying "natural" family time while weaving biblical truths into the conversation. It is the consistent impartation of these truths over time that makes an ultimate impact. Sharing with one's children principles for long life and prosperity will pay great dividends in time.

In fact, if I could be fatherly once again, I would urge my young women (for that matter, a young man or woman would benefit from this little word of advice) to carefully choose a husband (spouse) with a heart and demonstrated pattern of hands-on care for house, children and the "small things." If he can't do diapers, dishes or windows, run to the store, attend dances or sports events, (or if that has not been a pattern in his upbringing) be careful. It is not only hard to teach old dogs new tricks, but young ones as well. God has placed an extremely high importance on parenting well. One cannot afford to miss on this point.

Further, God's promise of a long life and the possession of His blessed favor (grace) are tied to (not caused by) our obedience to God's Word. I know for certain that long term fulfillment, prosperity, joy and eternal destiny are related to a joyful obedience to God's Word. Not the letter, but the spirit of God's Word, to love God with our whole being and our neighbor as ourselves (not self love, for the kind of love required by God begins as a gift and is operationalized by faithful choice). Whenever parents or spiritual leaders consistently apply love, though taken advantage of at times (part of living in this world, expect it but forgive quickly), God prospers us, and we will all sleep in peace.

Conclusion To The Beginning

From my heart and your mother's, to my precious daughters (and God's young adults who may have received this book as a gift from loving parents), we love you beyond words or deeds. Yet we know that the most important and sustaining loves of your life lie ahead. The love of a husband (or wife for you young men) is exhilarating and growth producing (iron sharpens iron), the love of children (which we hope you will be blessed with in His timing), will stretch you, devastate you, mature you, fulfill you. But most of all, more than a mother's love (which is immense), or a father's (unchanging and sure), is Father God's love.

It is time for your deepening walk with God. No one (not even me), can force you into a more intimate relationship with your Father, but if I could have one wish fulfilled, one desire satisfied, it would be that you know the Father as I do. No matter how much or little your bank account (much is better), how rapturous your spouses love, nothing in this world can compare to God's love for His children, and in turn you loving him.

Introduction

Finally, I hope that the fullness of the identity of Christ will be formed in you. If you really know who you are in Christ, your special heritage of faith, the unequaled privilege of kingdom living, you will fulfill your destiny. Your specific destiny in God will unfold over time if you will steadfastly hold on to Jesus. With this in mind, let's begin to look at a most important first step in Christian maturity and development; Christian identity.

Chapter Two

Identity — Who We Are

There are so many words which attempt to identify us. Beginning with our gender (male or female), and our personal name (Rebecca Ann, Rachel Elizabeth, etc.), there are many other names given to us which identify our roles or functions. They include American (or whatever), child, adult, wife, mother, father, worker, Christian. Only the last name (Christian) has the power to affect all other areas of identity. For to be a Christian, a true believer, requires a worldview distinctly different and infinitely richer than any other.

A secular worldview suggests many different things. It is primarily self oriented (man is the center of all things) materialistic (wealth and comfort are life's primary aim), pluralistic (many viewpoints and cultural expressions, all of equal weight), relativistic (there are no moral absolutes, only different strokes for different folks), and pantheistic or atheistic (there are many gods and all religion is a path to God, or there is no God, and humankind is all there is). This is a very simplistic summary. The whole field is worthy of intense study.

Much of this secular worldview or philosophical way of thinking about life, the world, people, etc., is dramatically opposed to a Theo centric or Christ centric (God or Christ centered) worldview.

A Christian belief system or worldview is based upon the historical facts of a personal and knowable God and His dealings with mankind. God through Christ created and sustains the entire universe, created all living things, created mankind in His image and likeness that we might rule over His creation. From the beginning, God has revealed himself through an ordered universe, a rational creation, and provided ultimate truth revealed through the birth, life, death and resurrection of His Son, the Lord Jesus Christ. There is no legitimate foundation for other philosophical systems of thought. Many other views, even differing religions, have noble truths and exemplary ideals, but none that compare to the majesty of the Word that became flesh, Jesus. All of history is summarized and given meaning by His life.

Of course, in our modern, post-Christian era, anyone who would openly claim that they know absolute truth (Jesus said, I am the way, truth and life, no man comes to the Father but by me) is labeled a fundamentalist, right-wing, Christian right, homophobic, charismatic fool. The world we live in believes that any worldview is assertable. Believe in psychics, ghosts, flying saucers, reincarnation, no problem, but if one dares to proclaim the truth of Christ as their worldview, condemnation will soon follow. This has always been the lot of people of The Book (Jews and Christians).

I still remember my first major encounter with the secular intelligencia. It was in my Introduction to Philosophy course at San Diego State University. We were studying all the great philosophers from Plato to the existentialists, with a special emphasis on Sarte and Hegel. I must admit, I have some difficulty following some of the logic of the writers, but did my best.

Our primary class project was to take one of the primary philosophers, expand and explain their beliefs, and make application through contrast to ones own life. I chose to write on Rene Descartes' attempt at a rational/logical explanation of God. I won't bore you with my approach, but my focus was to launch into an apologetic on the existence of God as revealed through Christ.

My professor was a professed agnostic of Hebrew heritage. He read my paper, gave me an A, and made a simple statement at the end of my report. He stated, "I have been down this road and have chosen not to believe. Sometimes I wish I could." I had to admire his honesty, but could not help but feel a bit sad that his worldview left no room for God.

My paper was not that brilliant, but my simple freshman logic presented a convincing apologetic. My worldview is that "The fool has said in His heart, there is no God."

The importance of reinforcing and expressing without shame your Christian worldview is essential. The more you do, the stronger it becomes. Our faith in God is both rational (ultimately, the most rational), based upon historical facts (not some weird science), and is the only worldview that provides a safe harbor in the vicissitudes of life.

Personal Identity

Most of you reading this work have embraced the faith of your parents, perhaps years ago. You may remember the approximate day when you asked Christ into your life. From the moment of that decision, confirmed in your baptism in water, you have been imparted a chosen identity.

In Ephesians 1:4, the Word states,

Identity — Who We Are

> *"Just as He chose us in him before the foundation of the world, that we would be holy and blameless before him."*

Further, in Romans 8:15 it says,

> *"For you have not received a spirit of slavery leading to fear again, but you have received a spirit of adoption as sons by which we cry out, 'Abba! Father!'"*

And in Galatians 4:5,

> *"So that He might redeem those who were under the Law, that we might receive the adoption as sons."*

The apostle Paul describes our identity in terms of adoption. Adoption, however, was not of newborn or infants, but for the mature. When a child was adopted, he/she was brought before the father in a public forum, where proclamation was made that the old was gone (old name, history, etc.) and the new identity and name now belonged to the newly adopted son. With adoption came all the rights of inheritance, protection, provision, love and security of a natural child.

Now this is very important. As a Christian, you belong to God. He is your Father, your Maker, your Lord and your King. He deserves praise and worship and above all else, obedience to His Word. Though he deserves all the above and could easily demand allegiance, He has chosen to allow us to choose him and His Word, or our own way. As a young adult it is time to evaluate again who you are and who's you *are. You really cannot be somewhat Christian any more than you can be somewhat pregnant. The time to make an unreserved total commitment to Christ is approaching. Yet I understand the difficulty in this. To deny ones own desires for Christ, to risk a call to Africa (unlikely!) to give up certain pleasures (few if any in reality, just the destructive ones) seems so problematic. Yet, since you clearly know the truth of your identity, to not take up the cross (your purpose) and follow Christ fully would be cheating both you and God. The Christian identity as defined by God cannot be topped by any other. As Christians we are saints with heaven as our destiny, members of God's family, God's chosen, the apple of His eye, a new creation, royalty from God's perspective, eternally and totally loved, etc.*

Who are we? Who are you? A child of God; a Christian. There is no greater title, no greater life. My prayer is that you will fully embrace your identity, your heritage. Rejoice in it. Express its worth in your own unique style, and enjoy the journey with the Lord.

Identity — Who We Are

Chapter Three

The Goals of Life

Thank God High School is over. Moms' and dads' are so proud of your accomplishments. Wow, you're in a University and looking ahead to a very promising, though trepidacious, future.

I remember so well my late teens. I was so very unusual (I know, a statement of the obvious), in that I had a very clear idea what I wanted to be and do. My girls had a solid idea as well, for which I am grateful. Aimless wondering without direction can be a nightmare. You must realize, however, that you are not "normal" if you are absolutely sure of your direction. To have some direction, goals and ambition are all good, but must be kept in proper perspective. Misguided direction, ungodly goals or blind, self-centered ambition can lead to patterns of despair and destruction. Thus, it is important to consult our friend, the Word of God, for help in this transition to insure balance and correction where needed.

Trust

Trust is the foundation of life and relationship. With trust we move forward with assurance and safety. Without it, fear and uncertainty surround us. Healthy parents try to provide a faith filled, trusting home by being consistent in words and actions. Unfortunately, no parent is perfect, though their

The Goals of Life

intentions were no doubt good. This is to be expected. It is truly fortunate to have both a mom and dad in your life. Consistent patterns were made available. However, one has undoubtedly learned that no human being, neither parent, boyfriend, intimate confident or eventual husband can be trusted perfectly. We are all human. We can disappoint.

God knew that this would be our reality. The worldview of today would be to forever reach for that perfect union in love, marriage, etc., or abandon the chase and give in to cynicism and distrust. However, there is One who you can always trust, Who will never leave or forsake you. Thus, you can have your basic trust needs met through the fully trustworthy One; God.

> *Trust in the LORD with all your heart and do not lean on your own understanding. In all your ways acknowledge Him, and He will make your paths straight. (Proverbs 3:5-6).*

The first and most important goal is to know the security of God's love while realizing that only He has ultimate control of our lives. Humans have always tried to control the environment. For certain, God expects us to apply ourselves to work, responsibility, integrity, and relationships. However, putting your trust in the ultimate goodness and provision of God makes the most sense.

> *If God is for us, who is against us? (Romans 8:31).*

Putting your faith and trust in God is essential and most reasonable. But honestly, trusting God is not always easy, and most believers struggle with this fundamental reality.

Secondly, remembering that we are quite different (and who wants to be like everyone else, anyway?), from the norm, the world, the Kingdom of God is where our loyalty lies. As a member of the kingdom, made up of all true believers, past, present and future, we are called on and empowered by the Holy Spirit to live in righteousness, right moral relationships, and peace, tranquility in the middle of turmoil, and joy, delight. Only through Christ can any of us accomplish this. Our righteousness comes from Christ and is exhibited through our faithfulness to the truth. Our peace comes through the fact of our wonderful position in Christ. Our joy or delight comes through abiding in the presence of the Lord, through enjoying all He has created and given to us, blessings, and by delighting ourselves in the Lord…whereby the Lord will give us the desires of our hearts.

> *Delight yourself in the LORD; And He will give you the desires of your heart. Commit your way to the LORD, Trust also in him, and He will do it. (Psalms 37:4-5)*

In discussing goals, you can't forget the goal of God's greatest missionary, the apostle Paul.

> *But the goal of our instruction is love from a pure heart and a good conscience and a sincere faith. (I Timothy 1:5)*

Timothy was the "adopted" child of Paul; he loved him with all his heart. Paul gives vital advice to his son, which if followed would help Timothy in his journey.

The Goal of Paul's teaching of Timothy was:

Love, or agape, God's unselfish type of love, which flows from a heart purified by the Word of God.

A good conscience, which means being free from the past, through confession and repentance, and co-perception or having the mind of Christ. That is thinking as Christ would, from a perspective of love for God and love for our neighbors.

A sincere faith, or a faithful faith that is spoken, proclaimed openly and without shame or fear.

These are tremendous goals, obtainable as we apply our lives to living for God.

The Goal of Service

Another worthy goal is to fulfill our place in the world through productive service. Mankind is rarely happy with extended leisure. Having nothing meaningful to do is a curse. It is not so much how much money one makes or the level of position and power one achieves in life. It is that God intends for us to work, to produce so that we have something to give to others in time of need.

One of my prayers has been that my children would complete a University education, and receive preparation for a career as needed. This is not an absolute requirement, but since they are capable, the expectation is reasonable. Being able to work in a field of choice creates an atmosphere of satisfaction and an opportunity to be a blessing to others. Besides, when your old man and old lady (dad and mom), get to retirement age, you can properly "take care" of us, in the style we would like to become accustomed to.

The Goal of Friendship

Friendship is so very important. Good friends are hard to find. Once found, they should be cultivated, nourished and cherished. Friendship begins at home. Most Parents desire to be close friends with their children for their entire life. Siblings should be friends, and a parent's hope is that brothers and sisters will be friends for a lifetime. Ultimately, your future spouse should become your best friend. The most sustaining aspect of a long-term relationship is a mutual faith and trust in God and a committed friendship.

Friendship must be developed. It starts by being friendly, with some mutual interest and equality of giving and receiving. Any relationship where you have to do all the relating is co-dependency, not friendship. Any relationship where there are demands on you for certain behaviors, other than faithfulness in order to have a relationship, should be suspect at best.

However, it is important to remember that friendship progresses through stages, sometimes closer, sometimes more distant. A realistic goal is to have 2-3 intimate friendships at a time. Jesus had up to 500 followers, 70 truly committed disciples, and 12 apostles. However, there were 3, Peter, James and John, which were His inner circle of most intimate friends. Of these, He was most intimate (best friends) with John. More will be presented on this important topic later in this book.

To Know God

Finally, by far the most important goal in life is to know God. To know means to experience. Everyone experiences the Lord in his/her own way, but generally we learn to know the

The Goals of Life

Lord through the disciplines of the church. God loves you so. His greatest desire is to have His life flow through your life, His love through your heart, His thoughts through your mind. Knowing God is the highest pursuit, the greatest challenge and the fullness of joy.

Chapter Four

Disciplines — To Accomplish Our Goals

To complete anything of worth, like High School, takes discipline. Discipline means the willingness to give up something of less value for something greater or more valuable.

To delay the gratification of sexual fulfillment for the purity of marriage, and giving up short-term financial power for the long-term financial gain from a University education, are just two examples of discipline and its results.

There are many important disciplines necessary for success in life. For discipline to be effective it must be cultivated. Those disciplines that increase discipline in life are related here.

Discipline of Prayer and Praise

Prayer is communication or communion with God. Communion with the Lord can be formal or informal, but most importantly should be personal and frequent. Developing a prayer life is not difficult. It starts with an acknowledgment of our need, is sprinkled with appropriate praise, includes asking for things needed, and is enhanced when we pray for others.

Disciplines — To Accomplish Our Goals

The most important thing to do to cultivate and develop a prayer habit is to begin. Ritualistic prayer is not helpful, but habitual prayer is. Perhaps you can start with 10 or 15 minutes daily. From there, adding more time or frequency will enhance your intimacy.

Whenever we begin to draw closer to the Lord, our flesh and the devil will fight us. With persistence, we can develop a habit which will strengthen and sustain us. This takes discipline.

Discipline of the Word of God

God's Word is precious. In Psalm 119:105 it states:

> *"Your word is a lamp to my feet and a light to my path."*

In II Timothy 3:16-17, the apostle Paul states,

> *"All Scripture is inspired by God and profitable for teaching, for reproof, for correction, for training in righteousness; so that the man of God may be adequate, equipped for every good work."*

Obvious to every Christian is the importance of reading (devotions) and studying God's Word. This too takes discipline. In the Word of God we find the complete revelation, a mystery made clear and understandable, of the truth. Direct guidance for living life to its fullness is provided within its pages. When needed, and if we pay attention, correction and training is provided. Through the study of

God's Word, a life long endeavor, our maturity is increased until we are fully adequate, prepared for any eventuality. (See 2 Corinthians 3:6)

Thus, to study or not is not the question. We must study. However, for our study to be effective, it must be systematic and a study of the entire Bible, consistent, preferably daily and something we delight in. No matter how long you read, you will always discover new truth, and when applied it will bring positive change, conforming you into the image of Christ, becoming all God intended you to be.

Discipline of Relational Accountability

The apostle Paul admonished believers in the city of Ephesus that a part of growing up to maturity was learning to "speak the truth in love" (Ephesians 4:15). This is easy to say but hard to do. Most of us fall short of this ideal.

If you were a child raised in the church, you have heard and heard many things that you did not need to hear, such as gossip, slander, rumor, sinful responses, etc. The American church, especially charismatic ones, seem to specialize in tearing down others, criticizing and judging. This is not God's will or desire.

To learn the discipline of speaking the truth in love requires accountability in relationships. Knowing that your friends are helping you remain true to the Lord is a blessing of immense worth.

For example, if a friend begins to gossip, remind them of their commitment to speak the truth in love. This may be sufficient to cause them to rethink their course of action. If one knew that their sin could be exposed, they would be less likely to risk unseemly behavior.

Children

As a young person, there are so many temptations. Temptations are common to all people: the lust of the flesh (cravings, appetites of the body), lust of the eyes (selfishness, self-interest), and the pride of life (self-promotion, self-exaltation). One of the things that helped me overcome was my relationships within the singing group, "Children". (I wish I could say that I have always overcome, but I have succumbed more than I like to admit).

I had a covenant with them. The covenant was that I would look out for them and they would look out for me. We tried to be honest and open with each other, and if caught in an inconsistency or area of sin, we "busted" each other. Since we loved each other, and knew each other's weaknesses, rather than supporting each other's problems, we prayerfully tried to help each other overcome.

Again, we were far from perfect and frequently failed, yet we would have been significantly worse off without the accountability.

Independence in life or ministry is not the ideal. In fact, it is one of the biggest problems in Western life. God's goal for us is mutually dependent or interdependent relationships, based upon mutual respect, and covenant agreements held fast between one another. My hope is that you will develop the discipline of accountability in friendships. If you are popular, rich or powerful, people will tell you what you want to hear and excuse your inconsistencies or even sin. A true friend will tell you the truth in love and hold you accountable *to your word. That is the kind of friend that is closer than a brother.*

Decisions

Chapter Five

Decisions

Over the next 70 years or so, you will face many forks in the road. As Yogi Berra, the great New York Yankee catcher is purported to have said, "When you come to the fork in the road...take it"...as making a decision is inevitable. A decision in one direction or the other can make a major impact in your life course, thus, making wise decisions is wisdom indeed.

I do not know anyone, including myself, who has made every decision correctly. Try as we might, it is inevitable to have some regret or at least second guessing on various decisions made or not made. One of the greatest wastes of energy is worrying about what could/should have been.

It would be my hope that the major decisions or life's milestones, discussed in the next chapter, would be negotiated smoothly and with graceful competence. In this chapter you will see four primary components or prerequisites to making intelligent, wise and judicious decisions.

Know the Big Picture

I am sure you have seen commercials like "Life's short. . . grab all the gusto you can!" or "whoever has the most toys at the end of the game (life) wins!"

This prevailing worldview is both shortsighted and denies reality. No one knows how long they will live. Enjoying every day is certainly important. However, each day, linked together, is to be filled with purpose. What we choose to be, our purpose in life, will determine our decisions and ultimate direction. The actual choices we make will further determine if we fulfill our purpose, enjoy life, or not.

The best place to begin to know the big picture of life is God's Word. If you know the big picture, and God's general goals for life, you are more likely to make good decisions which will receive His blessing; a vital component of success in life.

How can you know God's will? Most of God's will and purpose can be found in His Word. Here are listed but a few of the keys:

1. <u>God's plan is revealed through creation and revelation.</u>

   It doesn't take a genius to look at the stars, a beautiful rose, or a child's face and see the marvelous designs of God. "A fool has said in his heart, there is no God," (Psalms 14:1). Unfortunately, there are many foolish people who deny the existence of God.

2. <u>God has revealed himself through His Word.</u>

   In II Timothy 3:14-17, we read,

   "You, however, continue in the things you have learned and become convinced of, knowing from whom you have learned them, and that from childhood you have known the sacred

writings which are able to give you the wisdom that leads to salvation through faith which is in Christ Jesus. All Scripture is inspired by God and profitable for teaching, for reproof, for correction, for training in righteousness; so that the man of God may be adequate, equipped for every good work."

There is more archeological, scientific and historical proof of the validity and veracity of the Bible than of any other document/book ever written. Rational men and women have attempted to discredit the Bible. Yet, no other sacred book has established itself with more credibility in history.

Not only is God's Word reliable, but it provides wisdom, faith and is able to teach, correct and give direction. The Word of God reveals many purposes and patterns worthy of note and emulation, as seen in the many wonderful examples of what to do and what not to do.

In Psalm 119:11 it says,

"Your word I have treasured in my heart, that I may not sin against You."

In Psalm 119:105,

"Your word is a lamp to my feet and a light to my path."

Through the Word of God, the Lord speaks to us, giving direction and common sense for daily living.

3. <u>Most importantly, God has revealed himself through Jesus Christ.</u>

John 1:1,

"In the beginning was the Word, and the Word was with God, and the Word was God."

Jesus is the living Word. There is more proof of the life, death and resurrection of Christ than that Julius Caesar ever lived. Jesus proclaimed the reality of the Old Testament and eye witnesses were willing to die for the truth of Christ's miracles. The greatest miracle of all is that of the resurrection of Christ. By the power of God, Jesus is the only one to give up life and take it back again. Thus, He is our Lord, our Savior and the Christ of God.

God's Will is To Be Sought Through Prayer

Prayer, both formal and informal, is vital for spiritual growth and guidance for the future. Men and women from all ages have actively sought the guidance of God through prayer. Prayer is a vital link of communication between God and man. It is powerful and effective.

As a family, we were not always the best or most consistent at prayer. I blame myself for this. I should have been more consistent and persistent. Nonetheless, if I could advise what I have attempted for myself, and found to be most useful, it would be this. Pray everyday, and in every way found in God's Word. This includes:

Personal, Devotional Prayer

Jesus told His disciples that when they pray (daily, sometimes 3 times per day) they were to enter into their prayer closet, a quiet place, alone with the Lord, to pray to the Lord who listens to us in the secret place, and then answers openly, gives guidance, makes provision, helps in times of need for everyone to see. A time of personal prayer and praise to the Lord can become most gratifying. Thank him, pray for others, and ask him for your daily needs.

Prayers of Faith

> "And without faith it is impossible to please him, for he who comes to God must believe that He is and that He is a rewarder of those who seek him." (Hebrews 11:6).

It doesn't take tremendous faith, a firm conviction that what we pray for will happen, but just enough. Faith is not emotion; it is an attitude of certainty that our good God will keep His promises to us.

In Hebrews 11:1 it says,

> "Now faith is the assurance of things hoped for, the conviction of things not seen."

Essentially, faith is knowing that when we pray, we "see" in the spirit the things we ask for with an assurance that we will have it, assuming it is in God's will. Then, we wait with hopeful expectancy until we have the things we asked for.

The best example of faith is seen in small children, who have a trust in trustworthy people, an open heart, and a delight in life. The key to a life of faith and faith in prayer is to keep the childlike expectancy that what you need, God will supply...because God is good!

Prayers in Time Of Distress

I remember the time that Rebecca, my eldest daughter, was walking home from school. Three older boys were following her. She naturally became frightened, but boldness came over her. She turned on the boys and began to speak out loud in the Spirit. The boys, surprised by this "unusual" confrontation took off the other way.

The Bible states that, "Whosoever calls upon the name of the Lord shall be delivered, saved, made safe, made whole.

There will be times that people will be tempted or in trouble, often due to circumstances, sometimes of our own doing, sometimes not. In any case, you can and should call, cry out to the Lord and He will deliver you.

Further, in I Corinthians 10:13 it says,

> *"No temptation has overtaken you but such as is common to man; and God is faithful, who will not allow you to be tempted beyond what you are able, but with the temptation will provide the*

way of escape also, so that you will be able to endure it."

God never sleeps and is able to hear us when we call. When tempted, should not be the only time you pray, but is one of the times that we must pray.

The Lord misses fellowship with all of us. We were made by God to fellowship with him. He is always available, ever present, all powerful, all knowing, and desires our intimate communion. I encourage you to pursue this discipline - it is a life giver for all Christians.

God's Will Revealed by the Holy Spirit

When someone, even at a very tender age, gives their heart to Jesus, the Holy Spirit takes up residence in our spirit to live forever. In John 1:12 it says,

"He was in the world, and the world was made through him, and the world did not know him."

Well, hopefully you did receive Christ, as evidenced by the presence of the Holy Spirit in your life. Later, for most believers there comes a time when a deeper walk with the Lord is desired, leading to the infilling with the Holy Spirit. This indicates the desire and willingness, which is most reasonable, (Romans 12:1-11) to give one's life over to the Lordship of Christ. This also makes available the power to witness through your life and words and access to the Lord's many gifts. Perfection was not a part of the package for any of us. In fact, we are all moving towards a goal, to receive *our prize (the upward call or heaven) and to grow up in Christ as we follow God's plan. Our journey in Christ starts from knowing we are already in him, by his grace, forgiven, loved, fully accepted, and heaven bound, so we can live without fear, knowing that the Lord is always with us, as he is in us and we are in him.*

It is hard to understand the Trinity. Great minds have debated this for years, but it is one of those wonderful mysteries of God that are clear, evident, true, and unexplainable. The third person of the Godhead, the Holy Spirit, is not a wind, He is not a ghost, He is not an essence or presence, He is a person (see Matthew 28:19; II Corinthians 13:14). As such, He has personality, intention of will, purpose. One of His main roles in our life is to guide us to truth, and provide direction for our lives. He is the one who tells us to do right when wrong is easier, often through our conscience. He tells us what direction to walk or action to take. His voice is never rushed, anxious, or condemning. It sounds much like your own voice in your head but says things which are so profound that you know you couldn't have thought of tha!. It is so important to get to know, listen to and follow the voice or leading of the Spirit to insure your successful walk. Just a few scriptures on the importance of the Holy Spirit and His guidance should convince anyone of our need for him.

1. *We are born again by the Holy Spirit (John 3:5).*

2. *We worship in the Spirit (John 4:24; Philippians 3:3).*

3. *We are taught by the Holy Spirit (I Corinthians 2:13).*

4. *We pray by the Holy Spirit (I Corinthians 14:15).*

5. *We walk (live) by the Spirit (Galatians 5:16).*

6. The fruit (character of our life) of the Spirit is provided to us (Galatians 5:22).

7. The Holy Spirit lives in us (I Corinthians 3:16).

8. We receive power through the Holy Spirit (Acts 1:8).

9. The Holy Spirit provides us gifts for the blessing of others (I Corinthians 12:14; Romans 12:6-8).

10. We build ourselves up by praying in the Holy Spirit (Jude 20).

11. The Holy Spirit writes God's Word, His plans and purposes on our hearts (II Corinthians 3:2-8).

12. We are to be lead by the Holy Spirit (Romans 8:14).

13. He is our helper (John 14:16, 26).

With such an important role and function in our lives, we need to focus our time and attention on knowing the Holy Spirit. He will help us to know God's purposes, will illuminate the Word of God to us, and assist us to be all God intended for us to be, or the definition I like better, help us to be who we already are in Christ.

God's Will through Commitment, Not Compromise

Being raised in the sixties and seventies, I faced, and too often yielded to, temptations that bombarded us. Smoking and drugs were no problem, but other more subtle compromises attempted to erode my faithfulness and godly character. In Song of Solomon 2:15 it says,

Decisions

> *"Catch the foxes for us, the little foxes that are ruining the vineyards."*

It is rarely the big things that snare us on the road of life, it is small things allowed over time that can erode our foundation and lead to serious consequences.

Compromise is so easy in the 21st Century. It is estimated that over 60% of all high school students and even a higher percentage in college, cheat on exams. Their justification is that grades are so important that it is worth the risk. The problem is, if we cheat at school, where else might we cheat? Lying, petty theft, gossip, using others, unkindness, thoughtlessness, taking the easy way, avoiding excellence, are all compromises that can have disastrous results, though often not immediate.

My encouragement is to look for these "foxes" and if you find one, kill it! Every time we compromise our principles, no matter what the reason, we weaken our resistance to temptation and move farther from positive decision making.

The opposite of compromise is commitment. The Bible is filled with examples of men and women who made a commitment, a covenant, and kept it, no matter what. Let me review some.

Noah built a boat over a 500 year time span, all the while preaching righteousness. Unpopular though he must have been, he became the envy of all mankind as he and his family floated on the water while everyone else drowned in their disbelief (Genesis 7).

Abraham left a land of wealth, pursuing a city he had never seen, based upon a promise of God. He never wavered in his commitment and God fulfilled his promise (Genesis 12:1-4):

> *"Now the LORD said to Abram, "Go forth from your country, And from your relatives And from your father's house, To the land which I will show you; And I will make you a great nation, And I will bless you, And make your name great; And so you shall be a blessing; And I will bless those who bless you, And the one who curses you I will curse. And in you all the families of the earth will be blessed." So Abram went forth as the LORD had spoken to him; and Lot went with him. Now Abram was seventy-five years old when he departed from Haran."*

Deborah was a righteous judge and a prophetess who would not stand by idly while God's people were oppressed. She led God's people to overthrow their enemies, and brought peace to Israel (Judges 4 and 5).

Esther refused to seek her own comfort, but faced her own death for the sake of others (See the book of Esther).

Daniel faced death in the lion's den, rather than bow to a false god. And the three Hebrew children preferred fire to compromise (Daniel chapters 1-3, 6).

On and on it goes, mixed with stories of those who did compromise, eventually reaping what they had sown, Aachan, Korah, Simon the Sorcerer, etc.

A heart filled with selfish ambition will make decisions based upon their best interest alone. To compromise is expedient. A person of commitment, refuses to sell out for something as trivial as porridge as in Esau's story in Genesis chapter 25, but makes and keeps commitments, even in the "little" things, and thus builds character. This leads to God's best and generally, better results.

Decisions Can Be Made, God's Will Found, In the Affiliations We Nurture

Friends… we all need them. True friends, ones who love us on our bad days and stand with us when others won't are priceless… and rare!

Your mom was such a friend for me. My mom and dad fit that definition as well. The hope is that you will continue to maintain a cadre of faithful and loving friends. To do so is both possible and necessary for a happy life.

Unfortunately, very few others in my life have been real friends. I do have some in ministry that love me, pray with me, and help me when needed. I have some, like Jerry Hom from High School that are closer than my own brother. They are a source of great value, blessing and strength. I am blessed to have them.

Growing up, I did not have many close friends. Those friends I had seemed very loyal. However, I found that friends within a similar age range and time of life had little good advice to offer me when a decision needed to be made. They gave loving opinion, pointed advice, but since they lacked a perspective of history, their words were as good as Homer Simpson's. What I really needed was a mentor (or mentors), a man or woman with wisdom, who I could learn to trust, and who was willing to hear my dreams and visions and give direction for their fulfillment.

Well, I wish I could say I found someone. The fact is, no matter how I searched, I never really did.

So hungry was I for a father (mentor), I settled more than once for a co-dependent relationship with people who proved unworthy of my heart. This hurt all of us, to my dismay. Nonetheless, the search is worth it, and finding a mentor is still a godly pattern. Joshua had Moses, Elisha had Elijah, Solomon had David as his father, the apostles had Christ, Timothy and Titus had Paul the Apostle. Every generation is to nurture, parent and shepherd the next. Every new generation needs the godly counsel of mature men and women of God.

Of course, the heart of a father is to have the honor to be a mentor for his children. But only God knows best who will have the specific grace to lead you to greater maturity in God. Thus, the prayer of a father's heart is that the Holy Spirit will guide you to just the right one, and protect you from the wolves who would hurt, use and discard you for their own gain.

Your affiliations are so important. Friends are necessary for social interaction, feedback, fun and fellowship. An intimate friend, especially a spouse, is a longing for all of us. I stand in faith that God will, with your cooperation, find the very best for you. For guidance, connection, direction and support, mentors are by far the best to give guidance without *malice, especially as you face the all important milestones just ahead of you.*

Chapter Six

Milestones

A milestone is a marker signifying that something of importance has taken place. Many events (high school graduation, first prom, etc.) are looked back on as significant milestones or accomplishments safely negotiated, hopefully, as celebrated parts of your early life journey.

Over the next few years, typically between now and reaching your full adult identity (age 28-30), several milestones will be negotiated by you. How you handle each one, to a large extent, will determine your long range future. Any decision can be re-done, but in the critical areas discussed here, the undoing can be most problematic and painful. Perhaps this discussion and fatherly advice will help you make an informed, eyes wide open decision, which will be a blessing to you and pleasing to God. You will not like all I have to say here. Please keep an open mind, grapple with the concepts. Ultimately, all decisions are yours. Both God and healthy parents trust you to make the necessary adjustments for your life.

College

Most high school graduates will soon enter the stage of a college career. Unfortunately, most parents (certainly we were not) are not wealthy enough to provide 4 years of private education. However, assuming adequate diligence in *high school, most youth can make it into a public university. In these universities you will face many challenges. You will find different worldviews, tolerance for every opinion and belief <u>except Christianity</u>. The work will be hard, your time will be crunched. Hopefully you will find enjoyment and lasting friends throughout your college life.*

College is designed to prepare one for two things. The most important purpose is to teach you to think. One of the main differences (and distinct advantages) of U.S. colleges vs. the majority of the rest of the world is the focus on liberal arts and humanities which force us to think.

Up until high school, in church, your friends and parents have attempted to tell you what to think. Regardless of what you are told, your college will attempt that as well. Every professor will try to persuade you to think as they do. This is natural. However, it behooves you to learn to analyze carefully the instruction given, and endeavor to ask the questions necessary to clarify and understand concepts and issues for yourself. Those questions include:

1. *What is the professor attempting to tell me?*

2. *What is his/her worldview and how might it affect his/her teaching?*

3. *How does what is being taught compare to what I have previously learned?*

4. *How might this teaching modify my thinking or confirm things I already believe?*

5. *If the teaching is contrary to God's Word and Christian principles, why might the professor have such views?*

6. *How am I as a student to respond?*

These questions, or ones similar to them, though certainly not exhaustive, will assist you in sifting, sorting, understanding, applying or rejecting the abundant amount of new knowledge that you will be bombarded with. As with anything, it is important to talk about what you are learning, as this will frequently help you with the sorting process. If possible, withhold judgment on what you are learning until you really know what you are being taught. Finally, don't be too alarmed if you occasionally embrace a belief or doctrine (teaching) that is contrary to or appears to be contrary to your mom or dad's beliefs. In your university education you are likely to shift back and forth between opinions until you settle on one (usually a few years down the road) for yourself. Most intelligent adults can handle controversial, even heretical debate, knowing that this is a part of your learning curve, and necessary for your long-term embracing of truth.

It is everyone's hope that your college education will eventually lead you to a meaningful career. However, try not to be in too big a hurry to get there. You need to enjoy your education, while focusing on graduating within a reasonable period of time, and with your integrity intact. In light of these last two criteria, perhaps a bit of advice might be in order.

1. *Study hard, play often, rest when you can. Keeping things in balance is a challenge, but worth the effort.*

2. *Remember the word "no." Just because a professor or a student has a sure fire, guaranteed money making machine with your name on it, you do not have to "sign up" to get a better grade. "No" is a perfect answer (or perhaps "no thank you") when*

someone is trying, purposely or not, to rope you into their sphere of influence.

3. Beware of things that sound to good to be true. They always are!

4. A good name is to be valued above gold. Though a short cut might be available, it is frequently too costly. Remain a person of your word, with wisdom and honesty; a positive reputation is far more important than a point on your G.P.A.

5. Avoid Sorority Houses, they are cesspools for the most part.

6. Guard your heart and your time, make time for God, church, and friends. And don't forget to call home once in a while and come visit... your parents will always be your greatest supporters.

Career

Most parents have high hopes that their children will master a career, or join the family ministry/business if possible. This may not be your will or God's will. It is a "parent thing." In any case, one day soon you will make a very important choice of where to work, perhaps if to work for pay, and where you want to be at age 33.

In spite of what you may have seen in your father, work is not the most important thing. Again, all things must be kept in balance. However, God created mankind with an innate need to accomplish, achieve, grow and produce. This is a principal of the Kingdom of God. People are really quite miserable, without doing work that is worthwhile, rewarding *and purposeful; in short, meaningful, unless socialized to be otherwise and having a welfare mentality,*

My hope is that you will enjoy success in your chosen field(s). Our world is changing so frantically due to the rapid technological advances of the day. Who would have thought that since you were born, someone could achieve a degree from watching T.V. or through the internet, shop by phone, or have a complete business in the home? Because of these advances, whatever career you ultimately end up in, you must be a life long learner, adaptable to change, and thoroughly versed in the technological changes that you face in your line of work.

It is not so much in what we do, but how we do our work that is likely to change. Staying continually informed in your field will be important.

Along with flexibility and adaptability, it is strongly recommended that you learn and implement, without obsessing miserably, strategies of success. These must be founded upon solid biblical principles and sound wisdom. Here are a few thoughts on the subject. If you ask a parent, mentor or pastor, they can give you many resources that can help as well (also, see the bibliography).

Get a Vision

The Lord has created us with the wonderful gift of imagination, dreams and visions. Each is important, but actually quite different.

I am a firm believer that vision, that clear picture of a worthwhile end result, comes to us from God himself. Habakkuk 2:1-3 and Isaiah 6 speak of this and are covered fairly well in my booklet "Catch the Vision."[2] A vision from the Lord to do something, develop or build something, etc., that is birthed in prayer, motivates you to accomplish greater things then you could ever dream or imagine. Dreams and imaginations are pictures that you dwell on, wishes you hope for.

Both dreams and imaginations can be fun, but are not necessarily strong enough motivators or accurate indicators of God's plan for your career. The Bible says that without a vision, people perish. That's why I would strongly recommend that you inquire of the Lord what His will is for your career, and get a vision for your future. Please remember, God is not a cosmic kill joy. He is not likely to call you to Africa or India unless that desire was already in you. Psalm 37: 4 reminds us,

"Delight yourself in the Lord and He will give you the desires of your heart."

God also desires your fulfillment, do not fear or avoid him and his input. God really does know what is best for you, not father, and He gives you tremendous latitude to choose your own direction. Thus, you need to choose wisely, seeking counsel as needed from others who have gone before you.

---

[2] Available from Vision Publishing, or on line (free download) at www.booksbyvision.com

Purpose

Whether you have a vision, dream or an imagination, or just a good idea born of an opportunity given to you, you are always responsible to make the best of it. All vocations, to be successful, require hard work, dedication and diligence. Your vocational success will be enhanced if you have a purpose for what you do. For example, my Rachel (my youngest daughter) demonstrated what a clear purpose can accomplish. She set her sights on becoming a cheerleader, and then the captain of the Cheer squad, and she did, learning leadership skills in the process which will last her a lifetime.

Your purpose can go from paying the bills to gaining needful experience for contributing to a greater cause. The greater your purpose is, the greater the potential fulfillment. Whatever your purpose is, it should always contain a component for growth or increase.

When the Lord said be fruitful and multiply, He also said to subdue or take dominant control of the earth. Growth, raises, promotions and prosperity are not guaranteed in life, since we struggle against a demonically influenced world system. Nevertheless, your purpose should always be to better yourself financially, educationally, spiritually, etc.

Your question should be, "How can I grow, become, develop into a leader, be promoted, gain favor, learn skills, and receive raises in my chosen field? To be mediocre is poor stewardship. Though success in any endeavor never happens overnight, if you set your sights towards it with purpose, and then plan for it, the worst that might happen is you fall short of your ultimate goals or even fail. Goals are important. Remember, a goal is when you break down your purpose into specific, preferably measurable objectives, such as, I will work hard to get a good recommendation which could lead to a better job by September 1st, etc.

*Every highly successful leader, business owner, minister, etc., has failures that they have learned from as a part of the soil in which they have planted their success. Failure and set backs merely become the **fertilizer** necessary for success to grow.*

Once your vision, purpose and goals are clear and written down, both short term, 6 months to 2 years, and long term, 2 years to 50+, you then need a measurable and logical plan to achieve your goals. This is where outside counsel from a mentor can be most helpful. Seasoned leaders in a given field have many years of life experience, thus they can help you be positively realistic and realistically positive in your planning. One danger is to plan too large or too small. If you err, err on the larger side. A mentor can help you evaluate to see if a certain goal is obtainable. For example, is it realistic in light of your University class load, to work full-time, carry on a part-time ministry and do all the above with a modicum of success? Perhaps it is; perhaps not. If you intend to graduate college in 4 years, how will you accomplish this? These plans, written down, made a part of prayer and frequently reviewed (daily is best), will motivate your mind and body to accomplish these goals.

In all your planning, when you set your heart towards something, give it your all. Being firm in your conviction is important, while remaining flexible enough to adapt or change. Whether your career is long or short, primarily as homemaker or bread winner, the Lord desires that whatever we do, we do it with all of our heart or with purpose and for His glory. A career decision is important, but how we function or grow in our chosen arena demonstrates the favor of God, and our diligence proves our cooperation with the Lord in living His kingdom principles.

Marriage

All mothers and fathers eventually have to talk about this. Most parents are highly protective of their daughters, especially because of how important you are to mom and dad. This is one of the reasons frequent discussions on the topic of the importance of marriage have occurred, both in terms of God's desires and expectations, and the importance of the decision to marry and to whom. Doing it right the first time, and hopefully the only time, is the sensible thing to do.

As young adults, you will make your own decision. And since I have written, lectured and preached so much on this topic, I won't belabor the point. Let me simply share my heart in regards to using wisdom in the (perhaps greatest and most important) decision of your life…marriage.

First, remember that marriage was and is God's idea (along with life, love, etc.). You did not invent it, though you are discovering this wonderful desire for yourself for the first time. God himself indicated that our relationship with him was not enough. He knew that one of the deepest desires for mankind was and is for companionship and true intimacy; physically, emotionally and spiritually. From the beginning God planned for one man and one woman to leave (say good-bye to loyalty, resolve any past hurts, gain a new perspective necessary for the new relationship, embrace the truth of God, even if contrary to the belief or opinions of a potential spouse, parents, friends or tradition) your father and mother, cleave (become fully bonded, totally committed, completely vulnerable and intimate) to your spouse (and no *one else to that level) and the two will become (grow into) one flesh (Genesis 2:24-25). This is God's ideal.*

Regrettably, because of sins consequences in the world, we will never totally achieve the ideal, but we should believe and work towards it. When contemplating marriage (and really before) leaving and cleaving must be thought through. Many a relationship has been hampered due to conflict with the priorities of marriage, how much time is to be spent with each other versus family of origin, etc. Many marriages start out on the wrong foot because one or the other of the couple were unable to properly say good bye to family of origin loyalty, or had such significant baggage from the past that the past became their present and potential future. Your hope will be to have a spouse who can and will, preferably seen well in advance, demonstrate a maturity to love you sacrificially, even as Christ does. That is, a spouse should be mature enough (not perfect, but grown up), to value and consider your needs and wants ahead of their own; as should you of their needs and wants.

Sadly, many men and women as well, (but to a lesser degree) in our society have been reared in families where seeking the good of others was not emphasized. If a spouse to be is more focused on him or herself, old friends, personal comfort, and selfish agendas, more than on God first and you second, you would do well to reconsider your decision. If he or she is not grown up yet, it will take a long, long time to see them mature; if they ever do. Many do not. Be sure of their ability to leave their loyalty to family, personal ways of doing things, friends, etc. and thus really cleave to you fully. You should be, after God, especially during courtship and the early stages of marriage, the most important person in their life. Your importance should be demonstrated at all times, not just when they need you or are afraid of losing you as a primary "possession". Thus you become one in unity without fear or past hindrances to be ashamed of.

You might be asking, how can I assure myself that my choice or potential choice is the right one? A great question! There are no guarantees, but here are some helps.

1. *Use your head, not just your heart. Romantic love is wonderful, but unpredictable, often deceptive.*

   In other words, we tend to see hear and feel what we want to, rather than what is. To a certain extent, this is necessary or we might never get together as men and women. However, do not allow yourself the luxury of not thinking with open eyes, ears and mind.

2. *Get to know your potential spouse's family, personal history, hopes and dreams...and look for inconsistencies. In a person's history are learned (often just below the surface, emerging under stress and crisis) patterns they have and likely will live by. The best predictor of present and future behavior (not a guarantee; people can change) is past behavior. Learn all you can before making the decision to marry.*

3. *Ask yourself, are they loyal, will they run away or shrink under pressure, do they try and deny responsibility if caught in a wrong or can they openly admit, repent and start the process of change? Can he or she forsake all others for me? Are they committed to God, church, have ambitions, a plan for the future, besetting sins (major problems yet to overcome), etc.?*

If the answer to some of these questions is yes, it does not mean you should drop them like a bad habit. It does say that these issues should be resolved, either through discipleship, counseling, or whatever, prior to a decision as monumental and permanent as marriage.

Receive pre-marital counseling, preferably before an engagement. Thus, you can figure out if areas of potential conflict can be comfortably resolved before you feel obligated to marry. Counseling should cover much of point 1 and continue until you have agreement on major areas of life; such as communication and conflict resolution, children or no, how many, work and career vs. stay home with children, who handles finances, who is responsible for planning, where to live, how decisions will be made, sexuality; its importance, and agreed upon activities, etc.

When and if things check out well, conflicts are resolved, and a covenant can be established (and again, written down), it becomes possible for a wife to properly submit (show respect) to a husband, and the husband to love his wife as Christ loves the church.

For many, the last person you desire to talk to about who you are dating or future marriage is the parents (as in yours). This is a big mistake. It is true that we do not know everything about you. However, we know you from a personal and historical perspective better than you might think. Parents have a unique perspective because they have married well or poorly, have been successful or not in their relationship, and desire more than anything for you to be happy and fulfilled in yours. Parents can be overly cautious, but can also have unique insights and observations which, if heeded, can help you avoid major pitfalls.

Marriage and family, probably more than any area, takes hard work, sacrifice, abundant love, forgiveness and outright courage to be successful. Thus, use special wisdom, pray with an open heart, eyes and ears to the Holy Spirit, and trust God to help you. It really is that important.

Type of Person

Another picture of the type of person one should look for in a mate can be seen in the creation story. In Genesis 1 and 2, we see the following:

First of all, the man (used here generically, for man and woman) enjoyed and spent time in the presence of the Lord. In other words, they had a personal relationship with God separate from and distinct from each other. One of the greatest difficulties and causes of future conflict occurs when one of the partners has to "carry" the other spiritually.

Secondly, the man worked. This should be a given. A lazy man or woman or one with unstable work patterns should be avoided.

Thirdly, the man in the garden did more than work; he cultivated and nurtured what God had him oversee. Marriage takes work; which includes careful, purposeful patience. To cultivate speaks of starting and finishing, doing things with excellence, not just for the pay check but because doing something well has inherent value.

Fourthly, he had knowledge of the Word (God's commandments) and a desire for further growth. The man and woman in the garden were both versed in the commandments of the Lord. Both knew of the importance of avoiding eating of the tree of knowledge of good and evil, and embracing the tree of life (knowledge alone does not always lead to correct behavior).

Finally, you need a man or woman who will protect you from the evils of the world and support you in your attempts to conquer, to keep the serpent out, because of a sense of duty and love. No husband or wife will do this perfectly, but these characteristics should be a part of the spouse you choose.

Church

The church has always been an important part of our lives together. Unfortunately, the church as it is known and expressed today is a far cry from the church that Jesus established. Nonetheless, being an active member of a local church is one of the social institutions which develop long-term stability for family life. What church to become involved with is very important. Here are the primary characteristics to look for in a local church, recognizing that no perfect church exists.

First, a local church, even a house church, should have recognized leadership. The Word of God establishes that His church was built on the apostles and the prophets, that is, the church was founded on a solid government of apostolic and prophetic insight. Working in most local settings is a pastor/teacher, or perhaps an evangelist, necessary gifts to the church, but inadequate to establish a church long-term. Consequently, it is important to be involved with a church that has a solid foundation and a clear vision. However, there is a caution that must be noted. The church with all vision but no positive and progressive structure will be exciting but never fulfill its purpose. A balance of the two is needed. Look for a church with good leadership, strength and stability, and yet with prophetic insight as demonstrated by reasoned evangelism and strong worship.

This leads to the second major requirement of a strong and healthy church; evangelism and discipleship. A local church which is growing by the addition of new converts on a regular basis is best for a number of reasons. First, with the influx of new Christians, the Great Commission of the Lord is being fulfilled in the local setting. Secondly, where there are new converts, and especially when there is follow-up discipleship, there is less focus on the petty needs and politics of church life (and haven't we all seen enough of that). New converts lead to other member involvement rather than personal preoccupation. Discipleship includes providing for the needs of the wounded that enter the church. As is clearly seen today, people who enter the church do so to meet personal needs, resolve conflicts, provide structure and support for themselves and their families. A church that has the ability and burden to assist with the needs of the walking wounded is a blessing. Be careful of churches that major in only one area of ministry (deliverance, counseling, teaching, worship, evangelism). Ministry must be made available for the whole family, from birth to the grave. The sophistication of the programs are less important than the quality of love and nurture, as expressed from the pulpit, in the Sunday School class and through the membership at large.

Third, a charismatic church is preferable to a non-charismatic church. Nevertheless, more important than the level of singing and worship, the expression of the gifts of the Spirit, or the oratorical gifts of the preacher, is the sound emphasis on the Word of God. It is God's Word that transforms us, when applied to our lives in obedience. Having an "anointed" worship leader and preacher is a great bonus, and highly recommended if available, but integrity in the ministry and solid structure in the local church is needed for the long haul. The church is more than the pastor. It is far more than the name on the door. Healthy church life is infinitely necessary for quality living in this sin sick world. Having a functional eldership for accountability and positive growth is a key.

Most important, our spiritual growth is predicated on faithfulness and obedience. From the beginning, the lives of the saints of God have been measured by the faithfulness of His people to follow the Word of God. The Bible states that we are not to forsake the gathering together of the saints. It is so easy, when one has been wounded by church leaders who were trusted, to avoid the church because of it. However, that never accomplishes growth. One never grows through the safe path, but through the rough and tumble of interaction with other "crazy and wounded" in the local church. Through the good and bad of church life God's children learn to live and grow in loving and supportive relationship.

My hope is that you will never give up on the local church. It is God's divine instrument for your growth and strength, support and service.

Chapter Seven

The Future

Time flies, whether you are having fun or not...so definitely have fun! Time gets away from us all. As stated previously, finding a balance between work and play, together and alone, is a life long task. On the one hand, we must seek first the kingdom of God, while remembering that every day has enough trouble of its own. (Matthew 6:33)

Therefore, live one day at a time. Stop and smell, cultivate, enjoy the flowers, a smile, a song, a book, a friend, your brother or sister or help someone in need. The list goes on. Living one day at a time however, must be balanced with planning for tomorrow and having a vision for the future. People who find this balance are ultimately happier. I hope and pray for wisdom for you. One thing is for certain and worth repeating, the decisions made today will definitely effect your tomorrows. Thank God for His mercy and grace, but try not to put God to the test.

As this book is brought to a close, there are a few items to consider as you face your future:

1. *Remember, you are a divine original, just the way God intended. From God's perspective, you are uniquely created and gifted for greatness beyond your dreams. Therefore, <u>dream your unique dreams.</u> Do not let anyone steal them from you. Dreamers and*

visionaries see things in the future, and act today to bring them to pass. You can do that; so dream well.

2. *Sharing your dreams, goals and visions should be done cautiously; they are only for the privileged. Do not make the mistake Joseph did (though he did so in innocence) by telling his unworthy and jealous brothers his dream, who then sold him into slavery for their own benefit. You need not be paranoid, merely cautious. Develop trusting relationships that are tested over time to share your dreams with.*

3. *In Matthew 6:22, the Bible states that if your eye is single, your whole self will be filled with light. My understanding of this passage is that our mind must be fixed on something without wavering; not being double-minded. That does not mean one will never change… we all must. However, keep your eye trained on your worthy goals, follow the light, the Word of God, and keep your focus fixed on Jesus (see Hebrews 12:1-2). In this last reference, the writer is expanding on the very thing that allowed Jesus to endure the cross for us. It was for joy. Not the joy of suffering, though there is a certain nobility about suffering well, but the joy of knowing that the pain was worth the gain. Thus by enduring, we can achieve our God ordained goals, just as a mother, who faces birth with trepidation and the birth process with painful dread, yet forgets its trial with the first look into her beautiful baby's face.*

Finally, be open to God for change. Remain teachable or coachable. In order to do so, we must conquer our pride, any remnants of rebellion, and develop appropriate submission in healthy relations, through willful submission to authority and knowing who we are in Christ. There are four scriptures which speak of this. They are provided here for thoughtful consideration.

> "The fear of the LORD is the beginning of knowledge; Fools despise wisdom and instruction." (Proverbs 1:7)
>
> "For the LORD gives wisdom; From His mouth come knowledge and understanding." (Proverbs 2:6)
>
> "Remember those who led you, who spoke the word of God to you; and considering the result of their conduct, imitate their faith." (Hebrews 13:7)
>
> "To You, O LORD, I lift up my soul." (Psalms 25:1)

The Future

Conclusion

My Heart to Yours

What can I say? I love you. I am proud of you. I trust you. I am here for you. You belong to God.

For all parents, having the privilege of seeing their children born, hearing their first words, watching their initial steps, rejoicing with successes and weeping with failures, infinitely enriches our lives. To laugh with our children, cry with them, argue with them, delight in them; the collective memory of our lives together becomes progressively better, our joy deeper, and longing for mature adult relationship, which will grow ever stronger, increases daily.

As an emerging grown up, frankly you have out done yourself. You will always be our little children. For my failures, they are many, I have already apologized. If any hurts remain, let's take the time to work them through. All of us are like the description found in Jeremiah 18, a little marred, seemingly useless in ourselves, but when placed in the Masters hands, are a work of art, useful, ready and of immeasurable worth.

The word which came to Jeremiah from the LORD saying,

"Arise and go down to the potter's house, and there I shall announce My words to you."

Then I went down to the potter's house, and there he was, making something on the wheel.

But the vessel that he was making of clay was spoiled in the hand of the potter; so he remade it into another vessel, as it pleased the potter to make.

(Jeremiah 18: 1-4)

www.ingramcontent.com/pod-product-compliance
Lightning Source LLC
Chambersburg PA
CBHW060852050426
42453CB00008B/956